W9-CGY-507

The Olympic Winter Games

THE OLYMPIC WINTER GAMES

GAMES

BY CAROLINE ARNOLD

A First Book • 1991
FRANKLIN WATTS
New York • London • Toronto • Sydney

Cover photographs courtesy of Dave Black Photography

Photographs courtesy of: Dave Black Photography: pp. 2, 8, 15, 16, 21, 23, 25, 28, 31, 32, 36, 46, 48, 50; The Bettmann Archive: p. 10; Wide World Photos: pp. 27, 34, 38, 40, 42, 44, 52, 56; Sportschrome, Inc.: p. 54; Gamma-Liaison: p. 55 (Michel Ponomareff).

Library of Congress Cataloging-in-Publication Data

Arnold, Caroline.
  The Olympic Winter Games / by Caroline Arnold.
    p. cm.— (A First book)
  Includes bibliographical references and index.
  Summary: A brief history of the winter Olympic games, with descriptions of individual events and profiles of several past champions.
  ISBN 0-531-20053-1
  1. Winter Olympics—History—Juvenile literarture. [1. Winter Olympics. 2. Olympics.] I. Title. II. Series.
GV841.5.A75 1991
796.98—dc20   91-4667
                                                              CIP
                                                              AC

CONTENTS

The Olympic Winter Games

Vreni Schneider (Switzerland), winner of the
slalom and giant slalom, Calgary, 1988

WHAT ARE THE OLYMPIC WINTER GAMES?

Since 1924, athletes from all over the world have come together every four years to compete in cold-weather sports at the Olympic Winter Games. The world's best skiers, skaters, and sledders compete with each other for medals, to set new records, and for recognition as the best in their sport. Their excitement and glory is shared by spectators on the sidelines, and, thanks to television, with as much as one third of the world's population. Everyone watches breathlessly as the athletes perform their difficult and daring feats.

Young Sonja Henie captivated the crowds
at the first Winter Olympics
in Chamonix, France, 1924.

THE FIRST WINTER OLYMPICS

Winter sports have been popular in cold-weather countries for thousands of years, where they developed from the need to get around when it was snowy and icy. Yet, when the first Olympic Games were organized in 1896, winter events were not included. In 1908, ice skating was put on the schedule for the first time; it was included again in 1920 along with ice hockey. These events were so well received that many people wanted to organize a separate Olympics for a variety of winter sports.

Among those against the idea of a Winter Olympics were the Scandinavian countries. They felt a Winter Olympics would diminish the quality of the Nordic Games, a competition held in Sweden every four years. Nevertheless, it was decided that there was enough interest to hold both events, and a festival of winter sports was organized. It was held in 1924 at Chamonix, France, in the French Alps. The Summer Olympics were being held in Paris that year, and the International Olympic Committee (IOC) members voted to call this new week of sports the Winter Olympics.

Three hundred athletes representing sixteen nations came to the first Olympic Winter Games. One of the contestants was an eleven-year-old figure skater from Norway named Sonja Henie. Sonja Henie was one of thirteen women who participated at Chamonix and is one of the few women to have won medals in the Olympics before World War II. In the beginning, most winter events were for men only. Women's speedskating was added in 1932, alpine skiing in 1936, Nordic skiing in 1952, and sledding in 1964.

The Winter Games of 1924 were so successful that the IOC decided to make them a permanent event. Like the Summer Games, these have been held every four years since then except during World War II.

Each Winter Olympics is held in a different country, with cities applying eight years in advance for the privilege of hosting the two weeks of competitions. Six years before the games, the IOC approves one of the nominees to be the official site. To reduce conflict with the Summer Olympics, the IOC recently voted to stage the Winter Olympics in alternate even years with the Summer Olympics. Thus, after the 1992 games in Albertville, France, the next Winter Games will be held in 1994 in Lillehammer, Norway, and then every four years after that.

WHO ORGANIZES THE OLYMPICS?

The eighty-nine members of the International Olympic Committee are in charge of both the Summer and Winter Olympics. They choose the location of the games and establish the rules of the various sports. The members of the committee act as ambassadors of the Olympics in their own countries. The current President of the IOC is Juan Samaranch of Spain.

Although there are 167 member nations in the IOC,

many of them do not have cold enough weather for winter sports. This has not stopped some warm-country athletes from participating, however. In 1988, for instance, there was a Jamaican bobsled team, a figure skater from Thailand, and a cross-country skier from Fiji. The largest number of countries competing has been thirty-seven. Only the United States, Britain, and Sweden have participated in every Winter Olympics.

Every athlete dreams of being among the best in the sport, and for those who win medals, this goal is achieved. For many Olympic athletes, however, the thrill is in having the chance to participate on an international level. According to the IOC, the true purposes of the Olympics are:

to draw the world's attention to the fact that physical training and competitive sports develop the health, strength, and character of young people
to teach principles of loyal and sporting friendship, which should apply in other spheres as well
to stimulate the fine arts
to put emphasis on sports as games and distractions rather than as commercial business, and to show that the devotion applied to sports is an end in itself, not a means toward material gain

The Latin motto of the Olympics, *Citius, Altius, Fortius,* which means "Faster, Higher, Braver," embodies the Olympic goal.

THE OPENING CEREMONIES

Like the Summer Games, the Winter Olympics begin with speeches, a parade of athletes, and the lighting of the Olympic flame. Every year the opening ceremonies have become grander, thrilling audiences with their colorful pageantry.

After the athletes have assembled in the center of the stadium around their countries' flags, a short speech is made by the leader of the host country, who declares the opening of the games. Then, to a fanfare of trumpets, the Olympic flag is raised. The Olympic flag's design of interlocking circles is patterned after a similar design found on an ancient stone altar in Greece and stands for international sporting friendship. The flag's five rings also stand for the five parts of the world represented in the early Olympic Games (Europe, Asia, Africa, Oceania, and the Americas). At least one of the five Olympic colors—blue, yellow, black, green, and red—appears on the national flag of every country in the Olympics.

During the opening ceremonies, an athlete carries the Olympic torch to the top of the stadium and lights the Olympic flame. It remains burning during the rest of the games and symbolizes each athlete's endeavor for perfection and the struggle for victory. Then an athlete from the host country takes the Olympic oath saying, "In the name of all competitors, I promise that we will take part in these Olympic Games, respecting and abiding by the rules which govern them, in the true spirit of sportsmanship, for the glory of sport and the honor of our teams."

Juan Samaranch, IOC president, holds the Olympic flag
at the opening ceremonies, Calgary, 1988.

The slalom course at Calgary, 1988

THE WINTER SPORTS

Athletes compete for medals in seven sports at the Winter Olympics: Alpine skiing; Nordic skiing, which includes cross-country skiing, the Nordic combination, the biathlon, and ski jumping; figure skating; speedskating; ice hockey; bobsledding; and tobogganing, which is also called lugeing. Except for ice hockey and bobsledding, all of these sports have events for both men and women. In addition, several sports are performed as demonstrations.

No two ski slopes, cross-country trails, or sled runs are ever exactly alike and the snow and weather can change at a moment's notice. A skier's time down one slope cannot be compared to his or her time down another slope. For this reason, records are not kept from year to year in many winter sports events.

ALPINE SKIING

Alpine skiing tests a skier's ability to ski downhill as fast as possible. Although the skiers compete against each other, the real race is against the clock. Expert skiers control their skis with their whole bodies. The smallest shift in weight can change the skier's speed or direction. The clamps, or bindings, that hold the skier's boots to the skis are designed to unfasten if the skier twists too hard or falls. Ski poles are used for balance and turning.

The Alpine events include downhill, slalom, giant slalom, and the super giant slalom races. The Alpine combination event (downhill and slalom), which was held in 1936 and 1948, was discontinued for forty years. It was reinstated in 1988.

DOWNHILL

This race, like the sprint in track and field, tests the skier's ability to race as fast as humanly possible, sometimes reaching speeds of 70 miles an hour (112.6 kph). The highest average speed in an Olympic downhill race, achieved in 1984 by Bill Johnson of the United States, was 104.532 kph (64.953 mph)! Long, heavy skis and long poles help skiers reach such speeds. Skiers also work out in wind tunnels to determine their most aerodynamic position as they bend their knees and "tuck" their bodies. When not in a tuck position, skiers keep their feet apart and their hands out for balance.

Some of the great Olympic skiers of recent years include

Jean-Claude Killy of France (1968), Franz Klammer of Austria (1976), Phil Mahre of the United States (1984), and Marina Kiehl of West Germany (1988).

SLALOM EVENTS

In the slalom race, the skiers race on a zigzag, downhill course, turning at flags (also called gates) set in the snow. The skier may not knock down the gates or miss skiing around one. The course is usually about one quarter of a mile long (402 meters) with fifty-five gates for men and forty-five for women. The gates are spaced about 10 to 15 feet (3 to 4.6 m) apart and require about one turn per second.

Slalom skiers use shorter and more flexible skis than do downhill skiers. The sides of the skis have an hourglass shape which helps hold the ski in place for quick turns.

The giant slalom race is like the slalom except that there are fewer gates and the gates are spaced farther apart on a longer course. The super giant slalom race, which is even longer, tests a skier's downhill skills as well as the ability to turn quickly.

NORDIC SKIING

CROSS-COUNTRY

Cross-country skiers are the long-distance racers of the Winter Olympics, skiing on long trails over fields and through woods. Men's races include individual events of 15 kilometers (9.3 mi), 30 kilometers (18.6 mi), 50 kilometers (31.2 mi), and the 40-kilometer (24.8 mi) relay. Women's races are 5 kilometers (3.1 mi), 10 kilometers (6.2 mi), and 20 kilometers (12.4 mi) for individuals and the 20-kilometer (12.4 mi) relay.

Cross-country skis are longer and thinner than downhill skis, with bindings that attach only to the toe of the skier's foot. This type of binding allows the heel to move up and down in a walking motion. Except when coasting downhill, skiers move forward by taking long, sliding steps and pushing with their poles.

Skiers adjust to different kinds of snow by changing the wax on the bottom of their skis. In general, the colder the snow, the lighter the wax. In "freestyle" racing, the wax is not changed during the race. However, in the kick-and-glide type of racing, the skier might stop to rewax if there is a sudden severe weather change. Proper waxing helps the skier to gain traction for going up hills and to glide quickly down hills, sometimes at speeds approaching 50 miles per hour (80.5 kph).

SKI JUMPING

Ski jumping is one of the most thrilling sports to watch, as skiers shoot off the end of a steep snow-covered ramp, called the "in-run," and sail hundreds of feet through the air be-

Cross-country skier, Calgary, 1988

fore touching ground. The sport began in Norway in 1860, and was part of the first Winter Olympics in 1924.

Ski jumpers compete in the 70-meter and 90-meter events as well as a team 90-meter jump. These distances refer to the minimum distance the jumper must achieve. The height and angle of the ramp may vary from one location to another, but both the ramp and the landing hill are scientifically designed so that skiers can't jump too far and risk tumbling forward. ·

Each skier takes two jumps, and is judged on both distance and style. The perfect landing is in the "telemark" position, with one ski in front of the other and the knees slightly bent. The winner is the jumper with the highest total score from the two jumps. The judges may award a maximum of twenty style points, deducting points for faults such as bent knees or an unsteady landing.

Ski jumpers use longer and heavier skis than do downhill racers. They also wear lighter boots with bindings that allow them to raise their heels and lean forward. Until the 1950s, ski jumpers flapped their arms to control themselves while in the air. Today's more aerodynamic skis, helmets, and skintight suits give the skiers smoother, longer flights.

The Nordic combined event joins the 15,000-meter cross-country race and ski jumping. Like the other ski jumping events, it is for men only.

Ski jumper soars over the crowd,
Calgary, 1988.

BIATHLON

This event, also only for men, combines cross-country skiing and shooting. It began in 1767 as a Scandinavian military exercise. In those countries these skills are important for soldiers patrolling snow-covered terrain. The biathlon became part of the Winter Olympics in 1960 and requires contestants to ski a 20-kilometer (12½-mile) course, stopping four times to shoot a rifle at a metal target 50 feet (15.2 m) away.

The difficulty of the biathlon is to be able to switch quickly from skiing, which requires endurance and strength, to shooting, which requires intense concentration and steady hands. Each person must shoot ten times standing upright, and ten times lying down. For each target missed, one minute is added to the skier's time. The skier who finishes the course with the lowest total time wins the gold medal.

SPEEDSKATING

Speedskaters race on skates with long, sharp blades around a large, ice-covered racetrack. Until 1988, when an indoor rink was first used, this event was always held outdoors and skaters had to contend with wind and temperature changes as well as each other. Now skaters race on both kinds of tracks.

The biathlon contestant carries his rifle on his back.

Unlike footracers, skaters race only two at a time and most races require many laps around the 400-meter track. One skater starts on the inner oval of the track and the other on the outer oval. Each time around they change lanes, thus making the race fair and equal in distance. Although the two skaters race against each other, they are also racing against the clock. Racers do everything they can to increase their speed, including wearing tight clothing to reduce wind resistance. The best speedskaters can attain speeds of more than 30 miles per hour (48 kph)!

American speedskaters have always done very well and have won more Olympic medals in this sport than any other country. Men participate in the 500-, 1,000-, 1,500-, 5,000-, and 10,000-meter races. Women skate in 500-, 1,000-, 1,500-, 3,000-, and 5,000-meter races.

FIGURE SKATING

Figure skating combines an individual's athletic and artistic abilities. Figure skates have shorter blades than those used for racing and have sawtooth tips that help the skater to stop and turn quickly. Both men and women compete in three

Champion speedskater Eric Heiden (U.S.A.) at the 1980 Olympics in Lake Placid

different categories: individual events, pairs, and ice dancing.

The International Skating Union (ISU) determines the way each event is to be judged. Each skater is graded with marks between zero and six points. The highest and lowest scores are thrown out, and the skater's final score is the average of scores given by all the remaining judges on the panel.

INDIVIDUAL SKATING

Up to and including the 1988 Olympics, individual skating events have been scored in three sections. The 2-minute short program, which requires the skater to perform seven specific moves, was worth 20 percent. The freestyle event allows skaters to perform a program of their choice to music. It lasts 4 minutes for women and 4½ minutes for men and was worth 50 percent. The compulsory, or "school," figures, in which the skater traces variations on a figure eight, was worth 30 percent. In the summer of 1990, the ISU voted to eliminate school figures from the world championship events and the Olympics. Now the emphasis is on performance, rather than pure technical skill.

Figure skater Debi Thomas (U.S.A.) performs her individual program.

PAIR SKATING

In this event a man and a woman skate together as a team, performing lifts and throws that require strength, gymnastic skill, and grace. The judges look for smoothness and the ability of the skaters to be mirror images of each other. Like the individual event, both pair skating and ice dancing are divided into compulsory and free-skating sections.

ICE DANCING

Ice dancing has been part of the Winter Olympics only since 1976. It involves the performance of traditional dance steps on ice and differs from pair skating in that the partners may only briefly separate, they may not use lifts or throws, and they cannot be linked just by holding hands. They must function as one intertwined unit.

ICE HOCKEY

Ice hockey is a fast, exciting game popular as a spectator sport in both Canada and the United States, where the ultimate prize for professional teams is the Stanley Cup. In the Olympics, the Canadian national team dominated the sport until 1956. Except in 1960 and 1980, when the U.S. team won the title, the U.S.S.R. team has captured the gold every year since then.

Each hockey team is comprised of six players, including the "goalie," who wears extra thick padding and a face mask to protect himself from swinging hockey sticks and flying

Pair skaters perform in perfect symmetry.

The referee puts the puck into play in a game
between the U.S.A. and the U.S.S.R., Calgary, 1988.

pucks. Players attempt to put the puck, a small, hard, rubber disc, into the goal by hitting or slapping it with their long sticks.

Hockey is frequently a rough game as sticks become tangled and players crash into each other at high speeds. When a player tries to interfere with an opponent's control of the puck, it is called "checking." Referees watch the play carefully and call penalties for such infractions as holding or interference. For a minor penalty, the player goes off the ice for two minutes and sits in the penalty box. A major penalty requires five minutes penalty time. When a team is short a player because of a penalty, the opposing team tries to take advantage and score. This is called a "power play."

BOBSLED

Bobsledding as a sport began in the 1800s in the Swiss Alps. The first wooden sleds were raced on icy roads and passes. Today's fiberglass and steel models look more like miniature rockets than sleds and can go faster than 90 miles per hour (145 kph) as they zoom down specially built tracks called "bobruns."

Olympic bobsledding, which is for men only, has events for two- and four-man teams. Racing a bobsled is something like riding a roller coaster down an ice-covered chute. After the team members push off and jump into the bobsled, gravity alone pulls them from the takeoff point to the finish line.

Spectators watch as bobsledders speed
down the icy run, Calgary, 1988.

Weight limits, including the sled and crew, are 375 kilograms (about 827 lbs) for a two-man team, and 630 kilograms (1,389 lbs) for a four-man team.

Bobsledders wear spiked shoes to gain traction for their running start. After they jump into the bobsled, the front man, or pilot, steers while the last man, or brakeman, controls skidding on the corners. In the four-person sled, the two middle men lean from side to side in the turns, helping to control the movement of the sled. On straight sections of the run, the crew members lean back and jerk forward, a motion called "bobbing," which helps them to gain speed.

Bobsledding competitions have been held every Olympic year since 1924 except in 1960, when the people at Squaw Valley in California were unable to build a bobsled run because of lack of time and adverse weather conditions.

LUGE

The luge is a one- or two-person toboggan, which, like the bobsled, races down a steep, ice-covered track, sometimes reaching speeds of 80 miles per hour (128.7 kpm). In order to reduce wind resistance, lugers lie on their backs and lean back until they are almost flat. Each run takes less than a minute to complete, with winners sometimes separated by only a few thousandths of a second. Each contestant or team takes four runs, and the times of all four runs added together determines the final score. Men compete as singles and in pairs; women race only as singles.

DEMONSTRATION SPORTS

In addition to the Olympic medal sports, other sports may be performed as demonstrations. These may be unusual sports or those in which only a few countries can participate. Dogsled racing, for instance, was a demonstration sport in 1932 when it was won by a Canadian team.

Curling, a game that resembles shuffleboard on ice, has been a demonstration sport several times, including in 1988. One at a time, team members use sticks to push large stones across the ice to a circular goal called a "house." This sport is popular in Great Britain, New Zealand, Canada, Switzerland, and the northern United States.

Other demonstration sports in 1988 were freestyle skiing, in which skiers perform acrobatic flips and ballet routines; several events for disabled skiers; and short-track speedskating, also called pack-style racing because the skaters race together in groups of four or six.

Freestyle skiing
was a crowd-pleasing
demonstration sport in
the 1988 Olympics.

Jean-Claude Killy skis around a gate, Grenoble, 1968.

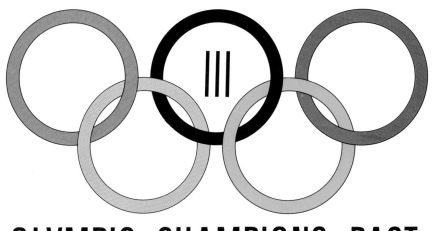

OLYMPIC CHAMPIONS PAST AND PRESENT

JEAN-CLAUDE KILLY, DOWNHILL SKIER

From the time he was a child, French athlete Jean-Claude Killy always loved speed. Nothing thrilled him more than racing down snowy slopes. Yet many things could have kept Killy from becoming a champion skier. During training he broke his leg and ankle bones several times. He also became sick and had to stop skiing for two years. Then, while in training for the Olympics, he became ill again. However, none of these setbacks stopped Jean-Claude Killy's determination to be the best.

The other skiers in the 1968 Winter Olympics were also very good, and each race was extremely close. Killy won the downhill event by only eight-hundredths of a second. Then he won the giant slalom. In the third race, the slalom, Killy's time was excellent and it seemed certain that he would win unless his main competitor, Karl Shranz of Austria, was able to ski faster. After a false start, Shranz also had a great run and at first it appeared that Killy had lost the gold medal. Then the judges declared that Shranz had missed skiing around two gates and disqualified him. Another skier beat Killy's time, but he, too, had missed a gate. Finally, Killy became the winner!

No other Alpine skier has won three gold medals in one Olympic year since then. As a former Olympic champion, it is appropriate that Killy is the co-president of the Albertville Olympic Organizing Committee for the Winter Games of 1992.

DOROTHY HAMILL, FIGURE SKATER

Dorothy grew up in Riverside, Connecticut, where she began skating when she was eight years old. She practiced for hours every day and was determined to be the best. Like

Jean-Claude Killy and teammate Guy Perillat rejoice after placing first and second, respectively, in the men's downhill race, Grenoble, 1968.

many people, she loved the creativity of free skating, but hated the discipline of doing school figures. However, she knew that to be a champion she had to do well in both.

Dorothy Hamill was nineteen years old at the 1976 Winter Olympics. She performed her school figures and compulsory program well. In her freestyle skating, no one had ever seen such grace and power. The judges gave her nearly perfect scores. One of Dorothy's innovations at the Olympics was a variation on a move called the "flying camel," in which the skater leaps and turns in the air and lands on one leg spinning. Dorothy added a sit spin to the end of this jump, to create the "Hamill camel." Her long hours of practice paid off when she earned the gold medal that year in Innsbruck, Austria.

THE 1980 U.S. ICE HOCKEY TEAM

When the tryouts for the 1980 United States ice hockey team were held in August 1979 in Colorado Springs, Colorado, players came from all over the nation. As in any other team sport, hockey games are won by teammates working to-

Dorothy Hamill in her gold medal
winning performance, Innsbruck, 1976

The U.S.A. men's ice hockey team celebrates an upset 4-3 win over
the Soviet team in the 1980 Winter Olympic Games.

gether. These players had never played together before, and in a few short months they had to learn to play as a team. They did this under the guidance of their coach, Herb Brooks.

In the Olympics, each team plays a series of games; the teams that win and score the most points go on to the medal round. In 1980, the most important game for the Americans was against the Soviets, a team that had beaten them badly in a game just before the Olympics. If the Soviets beat them again, they would be out of the tournament.

Each hockey game is divided into three periods that last twenty minutes each; after both the first and second periods the Russians were leading. But then, in the middle of the third period, the American team scored a goal to tie the score. Then, a minute later, they scored another goal to go ahead 4–3. When the final buzzer rang, the Americans had beaten the tough Soviet team. No one had thought this was possible, and when they beat Finland for the gold medal several days later, it was declared by sportswriters to be a "Miracle on Ice."

BONNIE BLAIR, SPEEDSKATER

Bonnie Blair, nicknamed Bonnie the Blur by one sportswriter, is the undisputed fastest American woman speedskater, having won five straight national sprint titles up to January 1990. At the 1988 Olympics she was twenty-three years old and one of the most promising members on the American team.

Bonnie Blair, gold medal winner of the
500-meter race, Calgary, 1988

Born to a family of skaters, Bonnie began to skate almost as soon as she could walk, but it was not until she was fifteen that she began to train seriously. Thousands of her fans watched as Bonnie waited her turn in the 500-meter sprint event at the 1988 Olympics. Her main competitor, East Germany's Christa Rothenburger, had skated before her and had already set a new world record. Bonnie knew that when her turn came, she would have to give the best performance of her life.

Bonnie was off like a shot at the start of her race. She sped across the finish line 39.10 seconds later, setting a new world record and winning the gold medal. Her winning time was only two one-hundredths of a second faster than Christa's. Bonnie hopes to repeat her performance at the 1992 Olympics.

BRIAN BOITANO, FIGURE SKATER

The only other member of the American team to win a gold medal at the 1988 Winter Olympics was Brian Boitano.

Brian grew up in Sunnyvale, California, and when he was eight years old his parents took him to a performance of the Ice Follies in nearby San Francisco. Brian was captivated by the way the skaters spun and leaped across the ice and asked to begin skating lessons. Within the first year he began winning prizes and developing a reputation for the skater with the highest and most daring jumps.

By the 1988 Olympics, Brian held several national championships; one of his main international rivals was the Canadian skater, Brian Orser, who had beaten him at the world skating championships in 1987. Their quest for the Olympic gold medal became known as the "Battle of the Brians."

Both Brians skated brilliantly in all three phases of the competition. At the end of the compulsory figures segment, Boitano was second and Orser was third. The next day, Orser was first in the short program and Boitano finished second. Going into the final freestyle event, Boitano was the leader, but only by a small margin. Whoever gave the best performance here would win. Brian Boitano skated first and dazzled everyone by flawlessly executing seven of eight difficult triple jumps. Orser's performance was also excellent, but because of one less triple jump and a tiny stumble, he came out with a slightly lower score. Brian Boitano said later, "It was my dream to win the gold skating my best. And that's what I did."

KATARINA WITT, FIGURE SKATER

Katarina Witt came to the 1988 Olympics as the defending gold medal champion. This graceful and glamorous East German skater, who is famous for her elegant expressive

Brian Boitano gives a nearly flawless
performance, Calgary, 1988.

technique, was also a six-time European champion and five-time world champion. Her major competitor in Calgary was the American skater, Debi Thomas, who had beaten her once at the 1986 world skating championships and whose strength was her superior athleticism. Both skaters had chosen the music of Bizet's opera *Carmen* for the final freestyle program.

Katarina skated first and instead of attempting technically difficult moves, enchanted the judges with her dramatic interpretation of the music. If Debi had been able to give a perfect performance of her more ambitious program, she would have beaten Katarina, but she unfortunately missed several of her jumps. Katarina's Olympic gold medal and 1988 world championship earned just a month later marked the end of a brilliant competitive career. Like many former Olympic champions, she now skates professionally.

MATTI NYKAENEN, "THE FLYING FINN"

Zooming down the ski jump runway at 54 miles per hour (approx. 34 kph), Matti Nykaenen tucks his body, puts his hands behind his back, and leaps into space. Soaring like a

Katarina Witt captivates the audience with her dramatic style.

Matti Nykaenen earns his third gold
medal in the 90-meter team jumping
competition, Calgary, 1988.

bird, it sometimes seems as if he will sail forever, and when he reaches the ground he has usually jumped farther than anyone else.

In the 1984 Olympics, Matti won a gold medal in the 90-meter event and a silver in the 70-meter. A 294-foot jump, in the 90-meter event at the 1988 Olympics at Calgary, won him another gold medal. Then, several days later he won his second gold in the 70 meters. Matti is a national hero in his native Finland, and his coach calls him the best ski jumper of the last 100 years. Matti began jumping when he was nine years old. In 1988, at age twenty-four, he was still jumping nearly 6,000 times a year. He says, "You must experience the feeling. It feels like flying."

ALBERTO TOMBA, KING OF THE SLALOM

Italian skier Alberto Tomba charmed viewers of the 1988 Olympics with both his outgoing personality and his outstanding skiing. He was always in good spirits and didn't seem to worry about his races. For instance, while waiting for his second run in the giant slalom, he left his teammates to call his family in Italy for a chat. He hung up, returned to the race, skied down, and won his first gold medal. Several days later he won a gold medal in the slalom as well, beating the second-place skier by a mere six-hundredths of a second. Tomba's powerful style is so smooth and effortless that he makes his winning performances look easy. His competitors will attest that they are not.

Alberto Tomba, above, turns expertly around
a slalom gate, Calgary, 1988.
Tomba, facing page, at the end
of a successful run.

On the last day of competition, the athletes gather once
again under the Olympic flame for the closing ceremonies.
Afterward, the flame will be extinguished until the
following Winter Olympics.

THE MEDAL CEREMONY

To receive their medals, the athletes stand on the winners' platform and face the official stands. The first-place winner stands in the center, the second on the left, and the third on the right. The president of the International Olympic Committee then gives them each a medal: gold for first, silver for second, and bronze for third. At the same time, the flags of the three winners' countries are raised and the band plays the national anthem of the first-place winner's country.

Winning an Olympic medal is one of the highest honors an amateur athlete can attain, and one which takes years of practice and training. It also takes determination and often a bit of luck. The moment in which the medal is received is one which the athlete will never forget. The Olympic Games provide the chance for great sports achievements by both teams and individuals. They also promote friendship among people from all over the world.

SITES OF THE WINTER OLYMPICS

1924 Chamonix, France

1928 St. Moritz, Switzerland

1932 Lake Placid, New York, United States

1936 Garmisch-Partenkirchen, Germany

1948 St. Moritz, Switzerland

1952 Oslo, Norway

1956 Cortina d'Ampezzo, Italy

1960 Squaw Valley, California, United States

1964 Innsbruck, Austria

1968 Grenoble, France

1972 Sapporo, Japan

1976 Innsbruck, Austria

1980 Lake Placid, New York, United States

1984 Sarajevo, Yugoslavia

1988 Calgary, Alberta, Canada

1992 Albertville, France

1994 Lillehammer, Norway

FOR FURTHER READING

Aaseng, Nathan. *Eric Heiden: Winner in Gold*. Minneapolis: Lerner Publications, 1980.

Greenberg, Stan. *Olympic Games, The Records*. New York: Guinness, 1987.

Hahn, James, and Lynn Hahn. *Killy! The Sports Career of Jean-Claude Killy*. Mankato, Minn.: Crestwood House, 1981.

Hamill, Dorothy, and Elva Clairmont. *Dorothy Hamill on and off the Ice*. New York: Knopf, 1983.

Ice Skating Institute of America. *Olympic Figure Skating.* Chicago: Children's Press, 1979.

Ice Skating Institute of America. *Olympic Speed Skating.* Chicago: Children's Press, 1979.

Litsky, Frank. *The Winter Olympics.* New York: Franklin Watts, 1979.

INDEX

Italicized page numbers
refer to illustrations.